Hurricane Katrina

TURNING POINTS IN U.S. HISTORY

Hurricane Katrina

Judith Bloom Fradin
Dennis Brindell Fradin

Marshall Cavendish Benchmark
New York

Marshall Cavendish Benchmark
99 White Plains Road
Tarrytown, NY 10591
www.marshallcavendish.us

Map by XNR Productions

Library of Congress Cataloging-in-Publication Data

Fradin, Dennis B.
Hurricane Katrina / by Dennis Brindell Fradin and Judith Bloom Fradin.
p. cm. — (Turning points in U.S. history)
Includes bibliographical references and index.
Summary: "Covers Hurricane Katrina as a watershed event in U.S. history, influencing social, economic, and political policies that shaped the nation's future"—Provided by publisher.
ISBN 978-0-7614-4261-5
1. Hurricane Katrina, 2005—Juvenile literature. 2. Hurricanes—Social aspects—Louisiana—New Orleans—Juvenile literature.
3. Disaster victims—Louisiana—New Orleans—Juvenile literature. I. Fradin, Judith Bloom. II. Title.
QC945.F725 2010
976'.044—dc22
2008038268

Photo Research by Connie Gardner
Cover photo by Michael Ainsworth/Dallas Morning News/Corbis
Cover: A young girl and her family wade through the floodwaters of Hurricane Katrina to find shelter at the Superdome, August 31, 2005.
Title Page: New Orleans residents await rescue on a rooftop, September 1, 2005.

The photographs in this book are used by permission and through the courtesy of: *Image Works*: Bob Daemmrich, 30; Jim West, 39; *Corbis*: David J. Phillip, 3; Reuters, 10; Mike Theiss, 12; Robert Galbirath, 21; Louis De Luca/Dallas Morning News, 22; Vincent La Foret/epa, 25; Smiley N. Pool, 26; Bob Crosin, 32; Irwin Thompson, 36; *Getty Images*: Richard Olsenius, 6; Roberto Schmidt, 11; Getty Images North America, 15, 42-43; Luis M. Alvarez, 18; Helifilms Australia, 35; *AP Photo*: Cheryl Gerber, 17; David J. Phillip, 24.
Timeline: Getty Images North America.

Publisher: Michelle Bisson
Editor: Deborah Grahame
Art Director: Anahid Hamparian
Printed in Malaysia
1 3 5 6 4 2

Contents

A tornado drops down on a prairie along the North Dakota/Saskatchewan border.

CHAPTER ONE

Natural Disasters in the United States

The United States is subject to several kinds of natural disasters. They include tornadoes, earthquakes, and **hurricanes**.

Tornadoes are rotating windstorms that drop down from clouds and touch the earth's surface. The United States is struck by more **twisters** than any other nation. The Tri-State Tornado of 1925 killed 695 people—the highest death toll from any U.S. tornado.

An earthquake is shaking of the ground caused by the breaking of underground rocks. California's Great 1906 San Francisco Earthquake claimed about three thousand lives. The New Madrid, Missouri, earthquakes of 1811 and 1812 were so strong that they caused the Mississippi River to flow

A man surveys the damage after the 1906 Great Earthquake in San Francisco.

backward for a time.

Hurricanes are huge sea storms that rotate in a giant circle. Hurricane winds blow at speeds of at least 74 miles (119 kilometers) per hour.

Disasters: Man-made and Natural

Disasters happen in various parts of the world from time to time. Sometimes people cause these deadly events. The 9/11 terrorist attacks were a man-made disaster. On September 11, 2001, **terrorists** hijacked four jet planes flying above the United States. The terrorists crashed three of the planes into crowded buildings. The fourth jet crashed in a field after passengers fought with the hijackers. About three thousand people died in the 9/11 attacks. It was one of the worst man-made disasters that Americans have suffered.

Some disasters have natural causes. For example, **tsunamis** are huge waves triggered by undersea earthquakes and other disturbances. In 2004 a tsunami drowned 230,000 people in Indonesia and other countries along the Indian Ocean. It was one of the deadliest natural disasters of recent times.

Sometimes they approach 200 miles (320 km) per hour. When hurricanes reach shore, their winds rip away tree limbs and roof shingles, turning them into deadly missiles. With most hurricanes, though, water is the biggest killer. Hurricane winds pile up walls of water that flood coastal areas. These **storm surges** drown people along the shore. A hurricane that

The 1900 hurricane that slammed into Galveston, Texas, killed thousands and left the streets littered with bodies and debris.

struck Galveston, Texas, in 1900 was the deadliest natural disaster in U.S. history. The Galveston hurricane killed about 7,200 people.

The United States has government agencies that try to predict and prepare for natural disasters. For example, the nation has an excellent hurricane prediction system. Scientists at the National Hurricane Center in Miami, Florida, monitor hurricanes. They do this with the help of weather satellites, aircraft, and radar.

The deputy director of the National Hurricane Center gives a televised update on Hurricane Francis in 2004.

When it appears that a hurricane may strike a coastal area within the next day and a half, the National Hurricane Center issues a **hurricane watch**. The agency issues a more urgent bulletin when a hurricane is expected to strike a certain area within the next twenty-four hours. This is called a **hurricane warning**. Hurricane warnings alert people in the danger zone to flee. They also alert rescuers to get ready to save anyone caught up in the giant storm.

Sand and rain blow through a Fort Lauderdale, Florida, parking lot as Hurricane Katrina makes landfall on August 25, 2005.

CHAPTER TWO

Katrina Is Coming!

On the afternoon of August 23, 2005, a storm was born in the islands of the Bahamas off the coast of Florida. At first it had no name. Over the next two days, the storm gained strength. On August 25, its winds reached 74 miles (119 km) per hour, earning it the right to be called a hurricane. The storm was named Hurricane Katrina.

On the evening of August 25, Hurricane Katrina slammed into southeastern Florida near Miami. With winds blowing at 80 miles (129 km) per hour, Katrina at this time was a Category One hurricane, the weakest kind. It toppled trees, knocked down power lines, and flooded streets. In all, Katrina killed sixteen people in Florida.

BY THE NUMBERS

Hurricanes are formed when warm ocean water evaporates and rises, and storm clouds form. Without warm water continuing to fuel it, a hurricane fizzles out. Hurricanes are divided into five categories, according to wind speed:

Category	Miles per Hour	Kilometers per Hour
Category One	74–95	119–153
Category Two	96–110	154–177
Category Three	111–130	178–209
Category Four	131–155	210–249
Category Five	more than 155	more than 249

This was a bad situation, but Katrina was just getting started.

While over land, Katrina weakened. This was just temporary, however. After crossing southern Florida, Katrina reached the Gulf of Mexico. The warm gulf waters provided Katrina with an energy boost. By Sunday, August 28, Katrina had become a monster. With 175-mile- (282-km-) per-hour winds, Katrina had become a Category Five hurricane—the most powerful kind. The area where Katrina made landfall would be in for a terrible bashing. Here was the big question: where would that be?

The National Hurricane Center issued bulletins warning that Hurricane Katrina was zeroing in on the New Orleans, Louisiana, region. This was

Hurricane Katrina is seen in the Gulf of Mexico in this satellite image from NOAA, the National Oceanic and Atmospheric Administration.

terrible news. With 460,000 people at the time, New Orleans was a major city. Counting the suburbs, the New Orleans area was home to more than 1.3 million people.

To make matters worse, New Orleans is a low-lying city. In fact, most of New Orleans lies below sea level. Water nearly surrounds the city. As Katrina approached, scientists knew that the hurricane would probably destroy some of the **levees** (walls) that protected New Orleans from flooding.

For years, scientists had warned that a hurricane would cause a huge disaster in New Orleans. An October 2001 *Scientific American* article declared, "New Orleans is a disaster waiting to happen." In October 2004, *National Geographic* ran an article called "Gone with the Water." It described how disastrous a hurricane might be for New Orleans. Now these predictions seemed about to come true.

On the morning of Sunday, August 28, New Orleans mayor Ray Nagin held a news conference. The mayor said that everyone should leave New Orleans because of the danger of the approaching hurricane. "I wish I had better news," Mayor Nagin told the city's people. "We're facing the storm most of us had feared. This is very serious. The first choice of every citizen should be to leave the city."

Most people in and around New Orleans got in their cars and drove beyond Katrina's reach. Katrina was more than 200 miles (320 km) wide, so it would probably cause damage far beyond New Orleans. People elsewhere along the Louisiana coast also **evacuated** their homes, as did residents of coastal Mississippi and Alabama.

The storm was on its way.

Mayor Ray Nagin and Louisiana governor Kathleen Blanco shared the podium during a news conference at New Orleans City Hall.

People waited in (and on top of) their cars for water and ice distributed by the Army National Guard.

CHAPTER THREE

The Thousands Who Remained Behind

In all, two million people in Louisiana, Mississippi, and Alabama fled Hurricane Katrina. Roughly half lived in or near New Orleans. However, hundreds of thousands of people remained behind—300,000 of them in the New Orleans vicinity. Why did these people risk facing this hurricane? There were several reasons.

Many people who stayed behind were poor. They had no cars in which to escape. In New Orleans, more than 125,000 residents were carless. The city had no plan to evacuate them. As a result, thousands of people remained in Katrina's path.

Many people who stayed behind were elderly and ill. They were in wheelchairs, were blind, or had other conditions that made them difficult to transport. Some were in hospitals and nursing homes that lacked the means to take patients to safety.

People also stayed behind because of pets. They were unable to take their dogs and cats out of danger. Rather than abandoning their family pets, they remained in their homes to face Katrina.

Many people knew little about hurricanes. They believed the warnings were **exaggerated** and Katrina would not

The Crescent City

New Orleans is one of the United States' most historic cities. The French founded it in 1718. The city's oldest part—the French Quarter—was built along a crescent-shaped curve of the Mississippi River. That is why New Orleans is nicknamed the Crescent City.

New Orleans is also called America's Most Interesting City. The flags of France, Spain, the Confederate States of America, and the United States have flown over New Orleans. Many people of French, Spanish, and African-American heritage live in and near the city. These and other groups introduced customs for which New Orleans became known.

For example, the French introduced Mardi Gras, a celebration held on the day before Ash Wednesday. Mardi Gras is like a big party. It includes parades, balls, and many types of food.

Around the early 1900s, African Americans in New Orleans helped create a new kind of music. It was named jazz, and New Orleans became known as the Cradle of Jazz. The city's jazz music, Mardi Gras, and tasty foods such as gumbo (a type of stew) have long made New Orleans a popular vacation spot.

Those who stayed behind: five people, one dog, and one cat await rescue in their flooded New Orleans home.

be as dangerous as predicted. They said things like: “We’ve had storms before, and we got through them.” Their lack of knowledge would cost some of them dearly.

For these and other reasons, large numbers of people did not flee as Katrina headed toward shore.

This collapsed house in Mississippi is evidence of the phenomenal power of Hurricane Katrina's wind and storm surges.

CHAPTER FOUR

Hurricane Katrina Strikes!

Katrina struck the Louisiana coast at 6:10 AM on Monday, August 29, 2005. The hurricane hit shore with a fury. Its winds were whirling at speeds of 140 miles (225 km) per hour. Over the next few hours, Katrina battered coastal Louisiana, Mississippi, and Alabama.

In places, Katrina produced storm surges up to 27 feet (8 meters) tall—nearly the height of a three-story building. Wind and water ripped off roofs, wrecked homes, and destroyed cars and bridges. People in Katrina's path were struck by flying objects and swept away by giant waves.

The hurricane claimed two lives in Alabama. In Mississippi the death toll was huge: about 250. A spokesman said that Biloxi, Mississippi, looked "like

Boats damaged by Katrina, stacked like a pile of broken toys

a bomb hit it" after Katrina passed through. The towns of Gulfport, Bay St. Louis, Waveland, and Pass Christian, Mississippi, were also largely destroyed. The storm surge along the Mississippi coast carried boats far inland and dropped them in odd places. One vessel floated up the runway of the Gulfport-Biloxi Airport. Another was found at the drive-through window of a fast-food restaurant.

Katrina devastated New Orleans, Louisiana. The hurricane's storm surge raised the water level all around the city. The water burst through the levees in some places. In other places, it flowed over the protective walls. At least four-fifths of New Orleans was underwater by Tuesday, August 30. The water was up to 20 feet (6 m) deep. Nearby Louisiana communities also suffered massive flooding.

As water rushed into thousands of buildings in the New Orleans area, people ran for their lives. Many families climbed onto their roofs. Some hid in their attics.

Water poured into New Orleans after this levee, located along the Inner Harbor Navigational Canal, broke under Katrina's huge force.

The water surrounding people's homes in New Orleans was not only deep—it was filthy. Garbage and dead bodies floated in the water. Swimming to a place of safety was dangerous, so most people stranded on rooftops and in attics waited for help.

Helicopters and boats were sent out to make rescues. Over the next several days after Katrina struck, the U.S. Coast Guard rescued more than 30,000 people. Other government agencies, as well as private rescuers, also took people to safety. New Orleans priest Luis Aponte-Merced later described his Hurricane Katrina experience:

Two women and a baby were airlifted from the roof of their house on September 1, 2005.

People Who Could Have Been Saved

Many people in New Orleans survived by going to higher ground, such as highway overpasses. However, some of these people died while awaiting rescue. They fell victim to heat, thirst, hunger, and exhaustion.

Thousands of people trapped in attics and on rooftops in New Orleans used cell phones to call for help. On September 3—five days after the hurricane—a thousand people in New Orleans were still making calls, begging to be rescued. By the time help arrived, some of them had died.

When we learned that Katrina was coming, three of us priests decided to stay in our three-story school across from our church because we knew that many people who couldn't leave the city would seek refuge there. About eighty people had gathered in the school when a nearby levee broke early Monday morning. Soon our neighborhood was under 10 to 12 feet of water. To escape the flood on the school's first floor, people ran upstairs.

Through our windows we saw people climbing onto the roofs of their houses. Some of them built wooden rafts, or swam, to get to our school.

We spent a lot of time on the school's roof, trying to get the attention of helicopters and sleeping there. At night you could hear people in the neighborhood screaming and dogs howling. Some people saw snakes and alligators in the water.

On Wednesday helicopters began landing on the school's roof and rescuing people. Eventually all three hundred people were rescued from our school.

Survivors were still being rescued more than a week after Katrina struck. A seventy-four-year-old man, Edgar Hollingsworth, was found barely alive in his New Orleans home fifteen days after Katrina passed through. Mr. Hollingsworth was in terrible condition, however, and he died two days later. By then the search teams were retrieving dead bodies instead of saving people.

This map shows the path of Hurricane Katrina as it traveled across the Gulf of Mexico and gathered deadly force.

CHAPTER FIVE

The Sad Numbers

Hurricane Katrina was one of the worst disasters in U.S. history. It killed about two thousand people. About 1,600 of them were in Louisiana—half in New Orleans and half elsewhere in the state.

The deaths were just part of the sad story. Thousands of people were injured, some of them very seriously. Thousands more experienced **trauma**, or emotional upset, by Katrina. They still suffer nightmares because of what happened.

Losing a home is one of the most upsetting things a family can experience. Katrina destroyed or severely damaged nearly 300,000 homes and apartments. Many months later, Katrina victims were still living with relatives or

Wall-to-wall cots filled the Austin Convention Center in Austin, Texas, where four thousand Katrina survivors were housed in the storm's aftermath.

in shelters. Some were living in cars because they had nowhere else to go. Many families lacked the money to rebuild their homes and businesses. About 150,000 people left Louisiana and moved to Texas because of Katrina. Thousands of others scattered across the country.

The year 2008 marked the third anniversary of Hurricane Katrina. By then, many New Orleans residents had returned. Yet the city's population was still only about 325,000—just two-thirds its pre-Katrina total. Will New Orleans ever again be the bright, lively city it once was? The answer is not yet clear.

The Ninth Ward in New Orleans became a devastated scene of destroyed cars, homes—and lives.

CHAPTER SIX

The Lessons from Katrina

A hurricane is a natural disaster. Yet Katrina was also partly a man-made **catastrophe**. Radio and TV broadcasts blamed government agencies for handling things poorly. “We’ve known about this for thirty years,” New Orleans radio broadcaster Garland Robinette said about the possibility of a hurricane flooding the city. “And the city, state, and feds did nothing about it.” Blaming government agencies for being slow to aid Katrina victims, Joe Scarborough of MSNBC called the situation “a national disgrace.”

President George W. Bush admitted that the U.S. government could have done much better. In a speech he made on September 15, 2005, the president said: “Americans have every right to expect a more effective response in a time of emergency. The federal government fail[ed] to meet such an obligation."

The Louisiana and New Orleans governments received plenty of blame, too. In February 2006 the Office of the President of the United States issued *The Federal Response to Hurricane Katrina: Lessons Learned*. Page 1 of this book discusses the "inability of the government—local, state, and federal—to respond effectively to the crisis."

In what ways could government agencies have done better?

To start with, the levees protecting New Orleans should have been built to withstand a powerful hurricane. They should have been both taller and stronger.

Katrina Controversies

The Katrina disaster stirred up bitter feelings in several ways. For one thing, many of Katrina's victims were African Americans. Numerous black victims of the hurricane claimed that rescue operations went slowly because government agencies did not care about them. They also pointed out that when disasters strike foreign countries, the U.S. government is quick to help. Yet with Katrina, the country did not rush to help its own citizens.

There are also people who say that New Orleans should be abandoned. They ask, Why should a city be rebuilt if it might just be destroyed by another hurricane someday? Its residents answer that New Orleans is their home, and they do not want to live anywhere else.

Helicopters dropped sand bags to plug the breaks in the London Avenue Canal levee.

Also, officials should have done a better job of moving people out of Katrina's way. Fleets of buses and other means of transportation should have been in place to take people to safety before Katrina struck. Special plans to evacuate hospitals and nursing homes should have been made. The Louisiana Superdome and other large buildings should have been equipped to shelter people who could not escape the city.

Two women had to sleep in their car outside the Louisiana Superdome in New Orleans.

Suffering in the Superdome

Two large **refuges** were established in New Orleans for people who could not flee from Katrina. About 30,000 people sought safety in the sports facility called the Louisiana Superdome. Another 25,000 took refuge in the New Orleans Convention Center.

However, conditions became very bad for the people in both buildings. There were food and water shortages. The electricity went out, and it became very hot inside. To make things worse, trash piled up and toilets did not work.

Rescues should have been done faster and more thoroughly. Victims such as Edgar Hollingsworth should not have had to wait two weeks to be rescued.

Following the disaster, victims should have been provided with emergency housing quickly. In addition, they should have received more aid to rebuild their homes and businesses. No one should have been forced to live in their car because of Katrina.

It is certain that the years ahead will bring more catastrophes to the United States. More hurricanes will whirl in off the sea. Tornadoes will continue to strike. Big earthquakes will shake the ground. The country may even experience another terrorist attack or even a volcanic eruption. Hopefully, Katrina

Stories with Happy Endings

One of the last people to be rescued from Katrina was seventy-six-year-old Gerald Martin. Mr. Martin was found in his New Orleans home eighteen days after Katrina struck. He had gone all that time without food, yet he somehow survived.

When Katrina struck the Oceanarium in Gulfport, Mississippi, waves swept eight dolphins from their tank out into the Gulf of Mexico. Aquarium staff feared that the dolphins had died. However, two weeks after the hurricane, they were found huddled together in the gulf. The dolphins were rescued and taken to a new home in the Bahamas.

Hurricanes Gustav and Ike

Was Hurricane Katrina a turning point? Have the lessons learned from Katrina been put into practice? So far the answer seems to be: maybe. On September 1, 2008, Hurricane Gustav slammed into Louisiana with 110-mile- (177-km-) per-hour winds. Thanks to improved evacuation planning, two million people fled southern Louisiana before Gustav's arrival. The hurricane claimed about forty-five lives in Louisiana—far fewer than the death toll for Katrina.

Several days later, on September 13, Hurricane Ike struck Galveston, Texas, with 110-mile- (177-km-) per-hour winds and a 12-foot (3.5-m) storm surge. Again, thanks to good planning, more than a million people had evacuated the Texas coast.

Hurricane Ike claimed more than seventy lives in the U.S.—still a low number for such a powerful storm. Yet despite the warnings, thousands of people refused to evacuate Galveston. Unfortunately, for some people Katrina's lessons have yet to sink in.

taught us to prepare better for major disasters in the future. As *The Federal Response to Hurricane Katrina: Lessons Learned* points out:

Houses built by Habitat for Humanity volunteers for Katrina survivors have been part of the recovery process.

Hurricane Katrina will undoubtedly be regarded as one of the most destructive, costly, and tragic events our nation has ever endured. Yet the true legacy of Katrina can be that [it] triggered a real and lasting improvement to our national preparedness . . .

We cannot undo the mistakes of the past, but there is much we can do to learn from them and be better prepared for the future.

Glossary

catastrophe—A terrible, horribly destructive event.

evacuated—Cleared out; emptied.

exaggerated—Not exactly true; made to sound more dramatic that something actually is.

hurricane warning—A weather bulletin warning people that a hurricane is expected to strike a specific coastal area within the next twenty-four hours.

hurricane watch—A weather bulletin informing people that a hurricane could strike within the next day and a half.

hurricanes—Giant storms with winds of 74 miles (119 km) per hour or more that whirl in a huge circle.

levees—Walls built to prevent bodies of water from flooding land.

refuges—Places of safety.

storm surges—Large waves driven ashore by a hurricane's winds.

terrorists—People who commit violent acts in order to make people afraid.

trauma—An emotional upset.

tsunamis—Water waves produced by earthquakes, volcanoes, and other disturbances that occur beneath or near the sea.

twister—Another word for tornado.

Timeline

1718—The French found the city of New Orleans

2005—Before Katrina strikes, New Orleans has 460,000 people

August 23, 2005—The storm that will become Hurricane Katrina is born in the Bahamas

August 25, 2005—Katrina's winds reach 74 miles (119 km) per hour, making it a hurricane; Hurricane Katrina slams into Florida and kills sixteen people

August 26, 2005—Katrina enters the Gulf of Mexico and strengthens as it heads toward the New Orleans region

August 28, 2005—Katrina's wind speeds reach 175 miles (282 km) per hour as the storm approaches land

August 29, 2005—Hurricane Katrina devastates New Orleans and coastal areas of Louisiana, Mississippi, and Alabama; search-and-rescue operations get underway

1718

2005

August 30, 2005—Eighty percent of New Orleans is underwater from flooding caused by Katrina

September 3, 2005—Five days after the hurricane, hundreds of people in the New Orleans area are still making cell phone calls, begging to be rescued

September 16, 2005—Gerald Martin of New Orleans is rescued; by this time Katrina has claimed about two thousand lives

2006—Rebuilding of devastated areas has begun; 100,000 families are still homeless due to Katrina

2007—Because of Katrina, the New Orleans population has dipped to 240,000, half of what it was before the hurricane struck

2008—The New Orleans population has climbed to 325,000, about two-thirds its pre-Katrina level

2006 *2008*

Further Information

BOOKS

Dudley, William, ed. *Hurricane Katrina*. Detroit: Greenhaven Press, 2006.

Fradin, Judith Bloom and Dennis Brindell Fradin. *Witness to Disaster: Hurricanes*. Washington, D.C.: National Geographic Children's Books, 2007.

Miller, Debra A. *Hurricane Katrina: Devastation on the Gulf Coast*. Detroit: Lucent Books, 2006.

Palser, Barb. *Hurricane Katrina: Aftermath of Disaster*. Minneapolis: Compass Point Books, 2007.

Rodger, Ellen. *Hurricane Katrina*. New York: Crabtree Publishing, 2007.

Torres, John A. *Hurricane Katrina and the Devastation of New Orleans, 2005*. Hockessin, DE: Mitchell Lane Publishers, 2006.

WEBSITES

For Hurricane Katrina information and pictures from National Geographic News:
http://news.nationalgeographic.com/news/2005/09/0902_050902_katrina_coverage.html

A National Weather Service site featuring Hurricane Katrina data and graphics:
www.srh.noaa.gov/lix/Katrina_overview.html

For a wealth of information on hurricanes from the National Hurricane Center, start here:
www.srh.noaa.gov/lix/Katrina_overview.html

Bibliography

Brinkley, Douglas. *The Great Deluge: Hurricane Katrina, New Orleans, and the Mississippi Gulf Coast*. New York: Morrow, 2006.

Horne, Jed. *Breach of Faith: Hurricane Katrina and the Near Death of a Great American City*. New York: Random House, 2006.

United States, Executive Office of the President. *The Federal Response to Hurricane Katrina: Lessons Learned*. Washington, D.C.: U.S. Government Printing Office, 2006.

van Heerden, Ivor, and Mike Bryan. *The Storm: What Went Wrong and Why During Hurricane Katrina—the Inside Story from One Louisiana Scientist*. New York: Viking, 2006.

Index

Page numbers in **boldface** are illustrations.

About the Authors

Dennis Fradin is the author of 150 books, some of them written with his wife, Judith Bloom Fradin. Their book for Clarion, *The Power of One: Daisy Bates and the Little Rock Nine*, was named a Golden Kite Honor Book. Another of Dennis's well-known books is *Let It Begin Here! Lexington & Concord: First Battles of the American Revolution*, published by Walker. Other recent books by the Fradins include *Jane Addams: Champion of Democracy* for Clarion and *5,000 Miles to Freedom: Ellen and William Craft's Flight from Slavery* for National Geographic Children's Books. Their current project for National Geographic is the *Witness to Disaster* series about natural disasters. *Turning Points in U.S. History* is Dennis's first series for Marshall Cavendish Benchmark. The Fradins have three grown children and six grandchildren.